The Distance
Between Us

Also by Fiona Sampson

From Seren:

Folding the Real (2001)

Poetry:

Travel Diary/Patuvacki Dnevnik (2004)
Pliind Realitatea (2004)
Hotel Casino [chapbook] (2004)

Other:

Writing: Self and Reflexivity [with Celia Hunt] (2005)
Creative Writing in Health and Social Care (2004)
Ha' ani Gir'i hartiva (2002)
The Healing Word (1999)
The Self on the Page [with Celia Hunt] (1998)

Translations:

Evening Brings Everything Back [Jaan Kaplinski] (2004)
A Fine Line: New Poetry from East and Central Europe
[with Jean Boase-Beier and Alexandra Buchler] (2004)
*Orient Express: the best of contemporary writing from
Enlargement Europe*, Vols. 1-7 (ongoing)

This book also appears in translation:
Romanian: *Distanta dintre noi*, trans. by Ioana Ieronim
Macedonian: *Dalechinata megju nas*, trans. by Magalena Horvat

Fiona Sampson

The Distance Between Us

For Michi
with best wishes,

Fiona S.

JML 06.

seren

Serenis the book imprint of
Poetry Wales Press Ltd
Nolton Street, Bridgend, Wales, CF31 3BN
www.seren-books.com

ISBN 1-85411-397-6

A CIP record for this title is available from the British Library.

The publisher acknowledges the financial assistance
of the Welsh Books Council.

Printed by Dinefwr Press, Llandybie.

Cover photograph by Marina Giannobi.

Back cover portrait of the author by Swithin Fry.

Contents

I
The Orpheus Variation   11
Cante Jondo   12

II
Love's Philosophie   21
The Velvet Shutter   22

III
Leda at the Lake   29
Brief Encounter   31

IV
Mid-journey   39
Path   40

V
In the Early Evening, as Now   45
Turkish Rondo   46

VI
Brief History   55
Hotel Casino   56

VII
In the Sleep Marquee   61
The Secret Flowers   62

Notes   69
Acknowledgements   71

For –

Бидете вечно гладни! Тогаш, веќе сте слични.

Always be hungry! Then you'll become like each other.

– Aleksandar Prokopiev

I

The Orpheus Variation

Who'd believe, meeting us now,
that once we saw daylight undress each other

our skin smooth and cool as tiles:
that our breath stirred the leaves

in each other's hair?

Cante Jondo

Empieza el llanto /de la guitarra.
The guitar starts up /weeping.
— Federico García Lorca, *Poem of the Gipsy Siguiriya*

Who's this?

Doves smoke a gully.

Follow the line
the pointing finger –

in the desert presence bares itself.
Its pressure on the sky
is envious
            delicate
and what must be said moves towards us
though we can't make it out
among the piled-up ravines.

Here are two people walking in a desert:

with a lift of her hair
                    his hand
all of it flows toward them,
bones thighs whatever the hills represent

then like a gully turning
everything flows back,

dark slopes
the alignment of sky.

Here they are.
Two people
just coming to a halt.
Their breath in the blue air is little puffs *hooff! hooff!*
as if they're making clouds

so high
        so far
day splits around them.

Meanwhile, in darkness,
                        the heart
a plump irritable plum.

                *

Desert-shadows are curtains first one side
now the other.
At Chinese New Year firecrackers everywhere, terrible,
                                wonderful
were all edge
like the blade of light:

sometimes these two are like this.
Or sometimes the white evening smell
of breeze.
Important for them to understand this. Because now
sun burns their eyes.

Remember this. Weeping pain.

What must be said
is far off.

Touch me.

Nothing moves, air moves.
Nothing's touched them yet.
This is the white centre
where everything
holds to itself

the slope opposite bitter with shadow

sky a blue split lung.

Impossible to touch each other
                              impossible
to touch each other here

the path breaking and coming back like a leaky signal,
shoes covered in dust.
My iris tenderly strokes your feet.

Imagine a woman,
a man.
Imagine their losses.
Sun lays them bare.

Under a stinging sky
city clothes are flowers falling.

Or imagine papers on a daylit table.
An envelope.
                The hand
sealing its long white lip.

Imagine the heart's life like this.

                      *

At noon some things are invisible.

Even in the wide desert light
we make out a halting darkness.

                              Guilt
burns a hole in La Posa's hand
as she tries to escape her wedding:
through the hole you see milky sky
the white filter of a bird's wing
your lover's skin turning yellow.

Shepherd who went to the spring
shepherd who came from the spring

remove the evil eye
from the one you put it on.
Virgin Mary
you with your hand and I with mine.

Far-off, a door slams against the intelligent light.

Mother of the Sorrows
who's the third in our bed,
who's lying in the ditch
dirty as a *cabra*?

You don't look me in the eye.

Stones fall against each other as you walk.
Maybe you're counting them.
Maybe they clap their wings together, *castanetas*.
Ai-ai-ai-ai
who's your new squeeze

who's that under your skin who's riding you ragged
                                    getting a feel for you
who slipped her wedding rocks under our feet?

In the desert
outside is also inside,
sky and stone come very close.
Shut us in like a parched mouth.

                          *

Ai-ai-ai-ai
here it is
            the grid of presence

dust hot in your nose
and what must be said
scratch-scratching till the screen weeps blood

I was at the hospital.

15

They will take out this
and this.

Midday
        turns.

Your eye
        turns yellow.
Doors and grilles
            close.

Miserere nobis.
My ignorance won't look you in the eye
at the ordinary name of illness,
its polished general ward.

But the body
        inconsolable

is the burnt mouth the closed eye
everything passes through;

a dry place on the skin.

Can I touch you?
Putting my hand into the wound of presence

because I don't doubt this truth
that is a lie,
that is an ulcer in clear sky?

– Only you were breathless. You knew
in the honeycomb of your cells.

Presence burns under our feet.
Light explodes black blades
along the mountain.

Who will cut you?

Of the twelve-fold choruses
I can tell you five,
five for the holy ulcers,
six for the night candles:
of the twelve times over
eight for the joys we cannot understand.
Of the twelve-fold mysteries
I tell you nine,
nine for the nine months' waiting

two for the figures on a burning hillside.

Somewhere below is a town
                              branchy with lindens.
There are streets and clinics
in the shadow of mountains

curtains, tubes
                the shadow of a man
whose turn it is to lie down.

In the desert, absolute light
bleaches every landmark.
To love is always to lose.

Two figures.

This is the uncertain line of story
the moving finger.
It is touch.

II

Love's Philosophie

In a Hall of Mirrors
self finds self. Repeated.
Reflection's a gilded cage,
words rustle furiously against it.
In gold frames one self
prints over another, one movement
sets another lurching the opposite way.
Meanwhile, susurration of language:
speaking, we trigger a chorus
of selves. Their mouths move in silence
stopped up with glass;
and we resist them
even as they meet our eye
as if they, or we, were guilty.

The Velvet Shutter

Think of it as a long repeat
starting from here. Polished shadows in the hallway,
a piano's lucent shellac.
                              Mirrored rooms
unfold, behind my reflected head,

the bright consciousness of money.

You might call this harmony.

Mother preferred to say
the way things fit is
                              elegance
the best deserving the best
the fine line, Mozart's conclusive beauty.

Such a gift, neighbours told each other

but cost glitters
in that thrown line of *sostenuto*

                              caught by the kid
practising endlessly, behind drawn curtains.

Cool rooms. Light arrowing the rugs.
Mother's a perfect stranger. Even the piano
half-sick, half-proud to be touched by her

passing hand brushing my hair.
                              Brushed silk.
Keep it up she murmurs
as if distance mutes her already.
Dolcissimo the upstairs tap
and scuffle of dressing pumps.

I turned away, turned inwards
to the fiddle's blind belly.
Blister-necked, sweat sour on my strings.

Starting –

From cold corridors,
the stranger in the practice mirror,
O Lord deliver me –

success was a prayer answered, transcendental,
a plane door sliding open
to tarmac popping with lenses, *Our Teen Medallist*.

I was a Story

in the high key of over-reaching.
At my Wigmore debut,
Mother's ring on a chain around my neck,
I hardly shook.
The bow is concentrated sweetness
                            they said,
and overnight the world was my pal.

                                  My agent
settles me in Hampstead near the Pond
with Professor Johnston and his wife and tribe
of Gifted Children:
she in ethnic smock,
he gate-keeping The New Novel,
evenings, in the egg-yolk-yellow kitchen.

Was I happy there?
                      I think so.

Odd how lazy the eye is, how it
                              slips about
till a prickle of light from a gilt frame
the white kick of curtain in a breeze
catches it.
                    Odd
how it lingers on disharmony,
broken patterns.

When a string breaks
pitches explode
                    spiral to silence
a flight of harmonic geese.

                              – Did you hear that?

            Home is where the heart is.
            Difficult to see myself this way,
            set on cruise control
                              like abandoned dogs
            or swifts,

            to think of my heart distended by significance,
            bursting with its muscle.

            Home's somewhere else.
            You want to know where?
            Try meeting your eye in the mirror.

Look.

It's the height of stage
allows the front row so close
I hear their breath
                    rustle
when I close my eyes to play

this wordless line

pulling down a shutter
on the vivid podium
unconscious dark below the balcony,
                              returning you
to the plush interior
of self

        a cushion of faces
on my lids.

                bringing it all home
                              – snatches of talk
                your hand on the table
                              a snail's nippled antennae –
                out of the long turbulence of applause.

                It's distance that brings you close,
                lets us see my self
                in you
                        your self in me.
                                        Light,
                shadow.

                        Home
                is the bare room of attention.

III

Leda at the Lake

A question we have to ask is when she consents to be
broken.

There is an axle, it is not his –

Draws a straight line through the circle is the line of gender
marking
her species marks her out or down as the crouched dog bares
its gums

in a radiance of feathers.
Blue mud under the hedge.

Her blue.

The instant of collision: not then.

Not now she prays. *Don't let it be now.*

In the perfect clarity
leaves falling through trees. White green white.
Afterwards: there is a flickering.

Afterwards   in the blue TV
when the story breaks her into completion.

In the midsummer paddock on your back turning

the sky is a wing flung out
over water.

This is inviolable how does she come to accept
beyond the register of fact
how the space gathers her

As if so much
could shield.

All of a sudden the film jerks and spools it is fast
it is very fast   Where is the space now
she can roll into roll her body heavy with it?

He bends a neck. Now. It is now

how all the summer garden (you are looking)
how the spandrelled
parasols of cow-parsley where the wood

green

how they pull this apart

her feathered dazzling flank *In the heat of the day*
the bees at her crotch

There is a wheel she has it under her arm
when she stops you in the garden
putting her hand out. Now

Never comes to rest whirring
raises a breeze which lifts her (long?) hair.

You put the coffee on the terrace.

You lay (now) the saucers side by side on the tin
you bring the sugar bowl. Now
Smoothing the cloth

to turn

the spoons   white   (now)   brightly
a movement of   humming   Now

Now Now

Brief Encounter

Scars on a map.

The distance between us
might be no more than fifty yards
under the proscenium arch
of a stairwell.

Might be no more than half an hour:
time stepped out of its daily clothes

every second febrile
as the hairs on a girl's skin.
Those almost-invisible sensors
stirring.

     Time told over
till detail wears away

leaving a distance between self
              and self
where relief blossoms.

Starting –

The thirteenth
is a difficult, unimaginative date.
But I'm trying to
          get to the truth,
that shabby theatre.

And it's evening of course.
In your imagination
         mine too
it's always evening
when the bogeyman calls.
When this happens: a look, grazing touch, something
astray like hair in the eyes,

evening changing shape
like you do in a fairground mirror.
Only this night was clear glass
not warped or smudged.

It tasted clean as sorbet,
as steel
which does not dent or pucker
                              on skin.

A kitchen knife can cut through distance
closing the gap
between the flats at the end of the street
and the doorway I'm waiting in.

Its blade has no shadow.

And the four lit top-floor windows
will not open
when someone
when someone runs down the street
shouting.

              The empty road's blindfold.

Choked with space.

I could touch my finger
to this blade's rim
of silence.

Starting –

              and
how to close this gap?
How bring *He* and *I*
into the same story?

A knife is a short cut.

He has a knife in his pocket,
each step he takes
thrusts it into the seam.

Time
        begins to strip.

Hand in his blouson pocket
– call it a saunter –
he passes
the stagey first pass
above the garden wall.

To be seen
is to be in transaction,
and I'm in excess of my skin just now
                                blue shirt

but he's still
                not here
not the inner here
not yet having
                my longish skirt.

Think of body heat.
                        The turn of a wrist.
Think of time revolving
                like a trick of the moon.

In a couple of hours
it will no longer be the thirteenth
but vivid morning,
alive
        lifting its second syllable
in surprise.

Moon-blade in his hand –
an explosion of *here*

Leaning against the doorjamb
                          leaning down
he asks
          Who are you?

– *Cut!*

Men
only attack if you show fear:
like wasps
          or stray dogs

and I don't feel afraid.

His breath on my throat.
His voice crossed with silver.

Sleepwalking in the alley.

The blade on my throat
is a wound
              in the present,
it's the precision
with which the distance between us
the distance between living and dying
is measured.

But all the time his quiet words
                          he's watching
are like a sputter of March rain
                          he's watching me
although it's not raining
                          on the contrary
the sky's quite clear beyond the streetlights

and my little round buttons give one
by one
and he cuts through the bounce of fabric

and I don't feel exposed I don't
feel.

     as we murmur like lovers
in the deserted stairwell.

Innocence
is believing this doesn't happen
– *Your Face Here* –
              until afterwards
which is when I'm walking fast
towards the police station.

And even now
something flickers
in the fast-moving hands and eyes
of bus conductors neighbours guys at parties

– *Cut!*

What did he do then, his fantasy
cut short

my life his veering off?

The threshold of the self's a large lit room.

When the knife wavers
the naked minute opens for me
and I run into it
           in cut-up clothes
shouting
at the night
        barelegged

Here! Over here!
         In the silent street
one window slamming up.

IV

Mid-journey

You're right.   To enter you
                                        or me
is to enter a forest
where everything's alive.
Leaves stirring with private gesture.

Presence is a vivid scent,
the eye a spy in a wooden hide:

moving through as if native
we find
how form opens to form,
bulb into fern into tree.

How life constantly turns outward –
unstoppable forest
bursting with leaves and tendrils.

If this sounds like a sketch
instead of a letter
tonight the forest's so full of shape and sound
I hardly know where to begin
                                        or end
do you?

Path

Breathe

Trees deal
deal come up flickering deal flip-flap
leaves on a dark cheek.

                        Dark
grasps lighter dark

whereas a path
(you throw out a hand to scratch)
is making space out of itself space

opening its side:
                        wound which is not-tree

where the green breathing of trees
the lurch of space

Where your hand going about murders dark

the sleep of space.
Your hand
            refusing.

Where white is an hallucination

elder flowers are white gasps O O
opening like stings.
Everything drunk down to the ankles.

This is the not-taken
where we are
trees flickering like candle-flames

                        the path
open-close of reluctance.

                    Breathe

*

After-sleep space between the suddenly
mechanical eyelid and world:
after a weekend's drinking I feel the depression
like a solid thing.
                  Gestures,
turns to the left.

                  Voices in the dark.

A child sleeping under the coverlet of voices.

All night, arguments in a train corridor, bang-rattle-
pop of the compartment latch
                        ne razumem. Explain

couplings hinges ratchets pivots busily

explain cables and bolts
scratch-scratching against skin.
Explain the length of a night-lit corridor vowelling vowelling.

The deep beauty is in fracture.

This is the way shank fits
to groove. This is the black oil

which is everywhere and not.

Za-zoooom. Under everything *the long retreating roar*
the long retreat under silky grey
under fields like groomed fur coming towards you
and away Over, over and

spending

Explain says the child standing at the window,
her breath making a morning fog.

*

Blue blond of headlights
making and unmaking darkness

                                        like a jigsaw
(your hand under Grandma's)
on the hall table beside the rose bowl.

In that house
light here and there with its ruler

a car engine closing its wings

while woodland moved
over the grass across the stream   moved

its thick fringe. Look

Up and
          up

look there
Tilt your head, it's all
in the angle of perception   This isn't the *a-b-c* classroom.

The child leans between gutters and gables   enunciating
the white world   annunciating *Look*

beyond the mown lawn the almost invisible
water searching about
                          its narrow gutter

(hair ties bloom in grass):
                          look
how it closes the space and draws shadows down over it.

V

In the Early Evening, as Now

In the early evening, as now, a man is bending
over his writing table.
                                    – Louise Glück, *Poem*

The lawn's in front of him:
a sly blackbird pecks sideways
and a bent twig moves like a compass needle. He's breathing
                                                        hard
with that indrawn rasp of concentration,
this outgoing whistle. Through tense lips.
Beyond this, beyond the view from the window,
is that further view in which the man
leans against the glass towards
names and persons we don't see.
He's attached to them
by filaments of painful attention they can't break:
they're a puzzle to him
and he works to solve them. Like the small-footed beetle
balancing its way from grass-blade to grass-blade.

Turkish Rondo

Where'm I from?
Depends who's asking.

London suburbs stop being London somewhere.

When I was a kid
Hillingdon was all low-rise reasonableness, red-and-white,
Mum's petunias vibrant camp.
                                        I go back
and nothing's changed,
china thimbles, cacti,
the heating *whumping!* on at four:

world *as it was*
                        is and ever shall be
the muddy rec
                        streetlights
a spoon slicing red jelly in a blue bowl

world without end
                        and all of it mine
wet hair after swimming
Friday-night chips out the newspaper
                                        Amen.

Where do I come from?
A childish question.
Its echo trailed down the window.

Dad got the Other Woman
– some office slapper – pregnant
while Mum was having Steve:

Mr Poopsie did a whoopsie
When it began to rain

he couldn't stand the stress
and went round the girlfriend's

Saw a frog in the bog
Ran all the way to Spain.

Steve, poor fucker, looks like him.

It's this loneliness meaning brings on:

we understand what matches
our intimate self
phenomenon to *noumenon*
kiss to mouth

This Is Your Life
as the actress said.

On days rain sheers the campus windows
I find myself
             shape-shifting
between the pen holder
and framed photo of the girls:

I'm ten
on my new chopper from Dad
                    racing Bazza
doing Georgie Best in the goal mouth
and Mum'll have a fit
but tomorrow my clothes will smell chemical, faded
                       and clean
because that's how I am,
foul-footed, nose-picking, arsey and all the same clean
because it's completely real, this is the first time

not wanked up one wet afternoon.
                   What
gives us form? The stories we tell,
the voice we tell them in
I reassure students

and my reflected face
floats over the vista of lawns and lighted windows

neckless
        predatory
                a Miró bird
a flying Dali eye.

                Yes of course I'm flying:
wide white house, two monsters in the up-and-over
                                        garage,
a hum of chrome round the breakfast bar.

How my fingerprints refract that hum.
The secret about money is
it does exactly what it says,
a story watertight
                as alibi.

Nobody our way said *Tariq.*
                        It was *Rick*
Rick of *Rick's Motors*
smart geezer bit pasty-face.

Red-and-blue bunting
dodgy deals on the hard-standing round back:
put in the detail. The moral's in the detail

like the last mouthful of pint
sliding back down the glass
so you can examine it

                        except you can't.
Because you're *there*
which is a different way of spelling *other.*

Behind the laughter-line moustache
Rick hated autumn.

Reminds me of home he said,
meaning public decay.
Meaning unstoppable ending.

What matters
makes you in its own image.

How when you're a kid
everything's crazy with perspective?
The sofa arm your whole foreground,
the climbing frame an endless upward weight?

Wish I could see where you
played as a kid.

In the absurd tweedy office
Soaper talked like a therapist.

Next thing I knew the humbling
                            gratifying
laying-on of hands on my career.
Soon we were up and taking baby steps
(shaky with emotion) along campus paths.

Lov-er-ly!
            Rick's pride when I got the job.
Family love cripples you with its directness:

Mind you visit your Mum when I'm gone.

Came to see him too,
propped up breathless as a fish
Hope you aren't smoking, our Al.

Mum sat me on the stool with the farty seat
saying *That'll be nice, won't it,*
Rick in the doorway
poker-faced with presents.

                            and it was:
'Appy Days, Bruv
as Steve likes to say after a pint or ten.

49

But what use experience?
Either you've got none or shit-loads of it,
spend it
or save it up to agonise the neighbours:
Want to see my snaps?

Only if I'm in them.

Dying, Rick took his story with him.

Visualise
        (as Amy used to say)
running at thirty from language schools,
                        friends' marriages,
the miserable bundle of thesis under my arm.

But I opened my mouth
when Soaper said *Migration Studies*.

                     That's Al for Ali, not Alan.
(*Williams* is more tricky,
"Mum's name" I say. Not exactly a lie.)

What would Rick think, filing his fingernails over the
                           Sunday sink?

I guess he understood
               how to sell a story

once upon a time
tea flubbing out of the family pot,
Turkish Delight in tins and little wooden boxes

stubborn, nervy, jokey, Mum
wearing slacks and a fag
All alright then?

Still, when Amy said *Honey,*
your stepdad, that Turkish stuff?
That's, like, people of colour, right?

everything shifted.

You tell your life
or it tells you.

O Mr Porter what shall I do?
I wanted to go to Birmingham and you've taken me on to Crewe.

Sometimes light grids the back of the seminar room
sometimes the side

but always
                      I'm pink and blue as a My Little Pony
a lapsed blond in poplin
                            and nobody says
(what being obvious must be stereotype)

ethnic Turks are ethnically Turk:

not (sweetly) *What percent?*

Thank God for the young, so busy with their own guilt
they miss why it is
they can't understand us.

Do you
        understand me?
Breaking through skin
to touch
        the experience?

Of course all of this is story:
clothes-horses, soccer, wide-screen TV.
Of course everything in my life's *in vitro*, inseparable, filmic.

Tell us a story, Jackanory.

Tell me
        what you'd like to hear.

Beyond the picture window
faculty buildings graze

                                among trees

and out of a listening dark
I gather my face.

VI

Brief History

Tumble of wings. The broken bird
faces nothing. It's a blamming of shoulders against panes,
wings, tail, bunched to the heart's bursting force;
a mop of black feathers in which blood fists and scrubs and fists
against pain.

Afterwards, you lift the bird and its eye's sealed
as if resigned to your weakness. As if resisting
the stillness which opens like glass to show
yellow silk creased at the lid, the blare of blood on a beak.
Pull a flick-flack stretch of wing and let it go.

Hotel Casino

Everything writes itself into the
book the skin of page the white

unknown:
            smudges
inky under eyes, under the reading line.

A lash moving against a cheek is a pointer
you could mouth it mouth the tenderness

chora
lips sweeping up every detail of you, belly

black beard black line of eye,

the park with its babies dogs
                                pensioners.

                    *

Fairground of browse and grab:
a park with tortoises. Kissing under trees.

Cartier-Bresson's bodies are spilled on lawns
in Westpoint and Istanbul. Murmur of kissing

in the dark of Kalemegdan.

Vous les jeunes. In fifth-floor darkness

the new red of the rail darkens and dries:
a packed apartment dark in which

pilot, student, Mafioso
                                music
falling like leaves.

*

Bleached skin like paper.
The tired yellow bear sleeps

in the big white bed:

white sheets a crumpled page, *signe*

de toi,
        signs of you in my body
on my skin.
                Smoked glass in the lift

in the refracted street a kiosk
in the yard a ladder
                    in the Metro –

smart, glossy – all falls apart
in mirrors of hair.

*

Disapproval like a gasp
outside this minute

the minute of presence before its image
closes on it
            before the circling of mouths

kissing their zero sums.
                    Before subtraction.

Comfort me with apples

lips closing on skin
juice springing across the tongue –

what is
obliterated?

*

A train's long regression:
flatlands sunlight cows

        the hand

moving away slowly,
        the relinquished hand
sliding on glass, are a continuing

touch and there are strings between them
strings of atom sensation symbol flying

the length of a concrete platform.

A smear of country beyond closed windows.

The star of broken glass.
Radiance of a taped pane.

*

The book of remembering of forgetting
fear.
      The wet white screen. Your eye mine

as if touching, dirt
scenting the skin. Sweat seals it

asleep grief-cold in a slick of hair;
language lies around abandoned

and my
      and my
           night-time-wardrobe useless heart
ticker-tickers yours

much that is forbidden touching cheek-bones gently
from the leaning walls.

VII

In the Sleep Marquee

Heat is not a straight line it is a vault
breaking away   opening

the body. A cosmosphere
for sleep voyages.

Heat's umbrella-wing
thrown like your arm   that burning line.

*

Beyond skin the space of a skin   opens:
flags open in bright wind.   Roar of a clean engine.

How to explain
the drag of space inward and out

sucking out the flame between us   flaming like a bird's
flung wing?

*

How summarise
that beautiful burn, the magnetism

between flame's foot and hair
closing   opening

the body   opening
the line of flight?

The Secret Flowers

Look.

Line opens its testament
its urgent revelation.
The mind's eye a perfect flower.

In the astonished street
your white shirt's a sail folded by wind.
Behind the fountain
polished winter branches
                              shoot out
rosettes bouquets frilled ribbons of here
to crowd your chest.

Your petalled throat.

Starting –

Pull back the curtain.
Hot-mouthed poppies.

A breeze enters,
the odour of bending grass
like a far-off lament.

The meaning of flowers is form,
is outward movement
moving out of nothing
to nothing.
                    Cell added
to radiant cell.

We return home,
that thump in the belly

fish-belly

as if the body of the lover

brings us back where we started.

A day-moon hangs agape in the corridor window
and eyes
        violet roses
press against me

in your hands in darkness eyes are
crushed
        night moths among the curtains
among the ceiling-shadows.

This movement through form.
This life-longing which,
sometimes rueful,
we feel as the impulse to love.

The sexed, secret, lived-in face
opening into sense
opening in light
in darkness

under the luminous sheet

the underworld where savage flowers grow.

What we desire
is to arrive.
We move as if towards rest

but life is motion,
animate
        as we are.
Patiently
I enumerate you: skin hair nails
your eyes' lit wetness.
Your bones and inner organs turn
towards themselves towards embrace:

here.

Trees flower in your face.
Their shadows are fingers.
Darkness, overcome me.

*

Outside,
the grotesque elegant city.

My thief's hand is under your lapel.
What did I steal?

Tree-shadow after tree-shadow
the unknown
walks in step with us.
We live towards significance,
it calls us in.

Word branches to word.
Read my palm
                    a life
changing itself under your eyes.

Your sigh
comes from far away in the Caucasus,
wind rushing across a continent.

Slowly, slowly
what is inward turns outward towards us.

Touch me.

Light rushing over the globe.

In the window
lindens sway their dark sweetness.
Streetlights in soft places
                              darkness between trees

your thumb a hook in my mouth

your mouth squeezing my lip
till it loses itself
till my mouth blurs.
                    Overcome me.

Body begins to clarify itself.
Touched, its form becomes
sense.

In the dark room your nipples,
concentrations of darkness,
shrink
            flex.
Two starfish crawl your chest –
when I bite them, they tighten.

Here you are.

Somewhere a wardrobe door slams.

Undressing you is opening light, darkness,
each time newly shocking.
I begin to sweat.

                    Why
do I think of meaning like a fish?
Its shine
            its slipperiness
the way it's all muscle,
fluid power.

You stroke the sensitive arch
of my thighs they open
like a vowel

your eyes under their lashes
entirely black
my breasts stretched and tender

setting the white enormous sheet
                              flying

when I lean over you
your lower lids rise over your eyes
your arms stretch out on the mattress
to hold it back
to topple forward.

Meaning multiplies itself
with every hungry bite we take.

Smelling the metal smell of wanting.

Hear me breathe
in the new quiet

evening sucking itself back from us.

A blind thumb rubs my belly-button.
Love's where meaning
comes to rest.
                    Where
are you?

My finger slides along the hidden skin
under your jaw
your too-big thumb
catches the gut strings and arches of my stomach

sobbing.

In the room gone heavy
in the bruise-shadow of curtains
stories open
with a whipping sound

we step into a skin
and it covers nothing

we struggle
the many-headed stranger
growing in our arms

out of and beyond our bodies

pulling truth out of our selves out of reach
into pain

through sky's hundred lift-offs   deep humming blue
your hands gripping my waist   a runway smudged
                         with roofs and streetlights
sky above and below us pale as bone as ash as snow
colour leaving your mouth

and
into the collapsing in-roaring room
and

through walls beds windows open or shut
through days opening closing like desert dunes
like doors

like water

through the long indifferent corridor.

Notes

There are several Spanish terms in "Cante Jondo". *Cante jondo*
and *siguiriya* are among flamenco's sombre forms: *siguiriya* a
genre and *cante jondo* ("deep song") a style. "La Posa" and the
two "traditional" songs which follow are allusions to folklore
from the mixed village of Mojácar, in Andalucia; where,
despite the Christian derivation of this material, women still
wore the headscarf until the 1950's. La Posa (The Espoused)
was a village girl who agreed to marry the sorcerer living near-
by so he would lift a plague which was ravaging the village.
Trying to escape, she prepared to poison the sorcerer while he
slept; instead she spilled the potion, which burnt a hole
through her hand. "Of the twelve-fold choruses" is based on
counting songs sung by Mojácan women to prolong con-
sciousness sufficiently for dying patients to repent and receive
absolution. *Cabra*, goat; *castanetas*, castanets.

The Balkans form a background to some other parts of this
book. In "Path", *ne razumem* (Serbian) means "I don't under-
stand"; the Kalemegdan, in "Hotel Casino", is the bastion park
above the confluence of the Sava and Danube rivers at
Belgrade.

Acknowledgements

I am indebted to the Arts and Humanities Research Board and the Centre for Modern and Contemporary Poetry, Oxford Brookes University, for a Research Fellowship in the Creative and Performing Arts which enabled this book to be written. I am also grateful to the Trustees of Hawthornden Castle for a Fellowship and to the Fundación Valparaíso, Mojácar for a Residency.

Sections of this book have been published in Macedonian in *Patuvacki Dnevnik (Travel Diary)* (Knixevna Akademiija, Macedonia, 2004), an edition of the work of the winner of the Zlaten Prsten for an international writer, and in the chapbook *Hotel Casino* (Ark Arts, London and Delhi, 2004). I am very grateful to the publishers of both books. I am also grateful to the editors of the following journals, in which extracts have appeared: *Leviathan, Poetry London, Poetry Review, Thumbscrew; Abalone Moon, Absinthe: New European Writing* (US); *Eurozine*; and, in translation, *Bulgarski Pisatel* (Bulgaria), *Helicon* (Israel), *Nashe Pismo* and *Koreni* (Macedonia), *Caiete International de Poezie* and *Romania Literara* (Romania), *Letopis Matice Srpske* (Serbia), *Ars Poetica* and *Kulturny Zivot* (Slovakia). Sections have also been anthologised in *Vilenica 2003* (Slovenia), *Who is Who 2003?* (Struga Poetry Evenings, Macedonia) and the 2004 Festival Anthologies of Maastricht International Poetry Evenings and the Romanian Writers' Union Ovidius Festival. Parts were first broadcast on TV5 (Slovakia), Romanian International TV and Radio Novi Sad and Vojvodina TV (Serbia). A Romanian edition of this book, *Distanţa dintre noi*, was published by Editura Vinea in April 2005.

Finally, this book has had the extraordinary luck to benefit from several ideal readers. Saso Prokopiev suggested the whole project. I would also like to thank Magdalena Horvat, Ioana Ieronim, Steven Matthews and Ewald Osers for their suggestions and support. My especial thanks go to Tim Liardet, for exhaustive readings; and Amir Or, who edited – and in doing so transformed – the book.